MOONCHILD

Poems and Reveries

ARNAB RANJAN

Copyright © <Published Year> <Author Name>

Made with ❤ on the Notion Press Platform

www.notionpress.com

Preface

What defines poetry?

One doesn't write poetry, one composes it. It's a song, a tale a feeling, an emotion or perhaps an experience. Moonchild constitutes of feelings and emotions. The verses are penned precisely not only to explain but also question about everything that goes inside our minds and hearts. The very fabric of soul is unknown to us and here we are trying to understand the universe and its laws.

CONTENTS

THE WONDERS OF THE NIGHT

Wonders of the night
Then there's wonders of the light;
Tell me, O lonely traveler
In which you shine so bright?

Trembling in the twilight
You gaze upon the sky;
Alas, the selfish dawning light
You think and question: why?

You stare in the horizon
Cussing and bidding farewell;
For the time has come when you shall
Know your place too well.

O the Star steals their thunder
Outshining them to dull;
For miles above and yonder
The traveler descends to sull.

You hear the blackbird mocking them
As you wish that they could stay;
But the ruthless one has once again
Chased the wolves away.

You sulk and cleave unto the breasts
Of vision as you fade;
For once again your time shall come
And you'll be marching your parade.

As the muzak of cosmos holds none against
their sight,
For he knows quite well in which he shines
the bright.
Ye be the rebeller, yet you frown upon your
right,
Tell me O lonely traveler, about all the
wonders of The Night.

BY THE RIVERBANK

Sky, The bluest of sky
With two little wings side by side
I was born to soar up and high
But alas! despite all, one by one were my
dreams denied.

Curious mind, a gifted mind
Numerous were the ideas and belief
When everything seemed possible and kind
They filled my mind with doubts and
disbelief

One by one did they pluck my dreams
Off my wings which they battered and
bruised
Like a flightless bird that gazeth from the
stream
And gazeth at his feathers ill-used

Featherless I remain now
Flightless shall I stay
Once what's stripped is gone, How
Like Dante, I'm lost in the dark woods, astray

A thousand of death do I die each day
And with each breath my will I exhale
Obstacles after obstacles lay scattered all over
my way,
So much so that of my dreams have I lost the
trail

Have patience for your time shall come
And cometh has it been since ages
For aeons and aeons will still it come
Until death has knocked a few many sages

I stand underneath the bough gazing at the
lake
With suffocation that suddenly overwhelm
With difficulty it seemed to me I breath'd
But easier would've been in that watery
realm.

Like a diver that dives deeper in search of
gold
I dove deeper in search of life
Like a fish I swam so bold
But the currents that passed cut me like knife

On the bed deep down I lay in abundance

Drowned in my sorrow and left alone in pain
Like a fading memory which passes with
much reluctance
Slowly I felt my strength adrift in vain.

There I remain untouched and swollen
In grief and sadness alone I finally soar
On the surface of the lake where I now float
dead and broken
Will the living still do me abhor?

IF I WERE

If I were a bird
I'd flap my wings until I touched the sky
And feel the air brush against me
Gently, as I fly through it.

If I were a fish
I'd dive unto the deep where the mysteries
are
No matter how hard the pressure pushes my
scales
As I swim through it.

If I were a cow
I'd stare deep onto the horizon and try to
philosophize
The various aspects of the universe
And for every thought I have I'd moo.

If I were a fox
I'd be the council of the Pride, the greatest
mastermind
And with my cleverness and sly
The braun and brains at tie.

If I were a chimp
I'd scratch my head and try to understand
What exactly am I trying to understand
When all I do is smile.

If I were a bee
I'd get to taste the most exquisite nectars
As I buzz around all day, working hard, no
pay
And sting the snatchers at bay.

If I were a dog
The little things would have made me happy
I'd wave my tail with happiness
And lick it on it's face.

If I were a cat
I'd just purr all day
And wait for my keeper to feed me
So that I could eat and then go back to hating
him again.

But alas I'm a human
Wretched in my own cause
Believe me when I say
I am all of them but none.

PROVIDENCE BEAUTY

Beauty, defined in absolute grace
Mistaking the striking pallor of Her face
Unable to hold in, my feelings ablaze
And I in you, in an entwined embrace.

From heavens above, till the hell below
Never did I stoop so low;
But realizing the fate that weaves my brow
Dazzling in light, Her ivory sheath of snow.

The eyes of pearl and emeralds She hold
Looking into which even the Gods unfold -
Twinkling like a child with a gaze so bold
She's the Devil to whom my soul I've sold.

And with crescent of her lunar lip
Whose curve makes even the boldest slip
As from my daydream I take a sip
Drowning into her beauty as I take a dip.

And drunk have I been of her smile
For which I've covered yet another mile
Sometimes the heat drives me vile

But I know that good things take a while.

And from the mountains from which cleft
The stream that flows down and deft
The star arises in between the mounds of
heft
Whose abundance falls as if prone to theft.

The ivory sheath that covers the heat
Of whose fumes make a blood ripped beat
Like a drop of blood on snow, her pallor
takes seat
Where the crimson sea and the settling sun
meet.

The wisest of wise demand clarity
But her beauty, my gents, is no charity -
Even the moral judgers fall to depravity,
For no human law can describe Her with
brevity.

DEATH

I dreamt a dream where I found myself in an
abyss
Craving for the touch of a hand and a long
lost kiss;

Stood there searching for an exit, my mind
quickly analysed
Perspiring through my consciousness I
completely felt paralysed;

Amidst all this, a feeling of tranquility held
my heart captive
I couldn't help but feel my conscience at
once becoming active;

I chased the tiny spark of light which almost
felt like dawn
But the more I sought the distant it felt, until
I realized its finally gone;

I broke through the barriers that
previously held me down
I looked around now waking up and gave

myself a frown;

The spark of light that I sought for me has
ran out of life force
The fading star burnt out in absolute content,
giving its spark back to the source.

<u>IF I WERE (v2)</u>

If I were an ocean,
Would I be able to reflect you
As you float by?
Thoughtlessly surfing into the aimless sky
As I drift back and forth,
Struggling to hold on to the gravitational push
and pull
Why can't I float too, so carefree in the bluest
sky?
There! Don't deprive the star of its
magnificent shine!
How could you have a silver lining whilst to
madness
is where I'm driving -
If only I could raise myself like the tallest
mountain
That kisses the sky, if only
I could bring myself to rise again.

If I were a cloud,
Would I pour my heart down to you,
Empty myself, my being,
Just to make you have your endless fill,

As you inconsolably repeat the same
expressions
Waving back and forth?
Oh look! You try to reach me,
Created a massive wave, but all in vain.
How can you so brilliantly paint the abundant
sun in your canvas
Yet fail to capture me in all exhilaration?
Let me hide it from you, but
It's futile you see, still
let's keep arguing at the top of our voices,
until
My emotions start to gather and with a rant of
thunder
I can pour down on you
And into the grand blue.

TOXIC LUST

Once upon a December night it was
Felt so warm instead of cold because
Drunk in thy beauty, entwined in thy charm
Struck my heart, and caused me so harm.

In my mind, Oh ask me not
Haven't I ever unveiled that beauty?
For whenever I chanced upon you a thought
Always found myself so guilty.

Oh the curves, that hourglass silhouette
Enchanted my mind into a sophisticated
trance,
Forever and ever have I dreamt so wet
With hundreds of mannequins have I shared
my dance.

Drowning further deep in that orb
Pang did I feel not in heart but my loin
Alas the uninvited member gave a throb
For in the everlasting heat everything seemed
to be growin'.

Oh growing it was, mine love for thou
Although convicted was I in thy orbs that
shineth so bright;
For my love greeted you, without a bow
So much so that it gave me a fright.

Carnal instincts seeped my mind
Like a wild animal with aroused sense,
Taking your hand in mine I bind
Albeit the conflict, the drama didn't lose its
essence.

O dramatical was the situation, not I
For I am not worthy of such essence,
Beads of diamond caught my eye
For it was the cold perspire which did
condense.

The sparks of beauty crackled so bright
Like the eternal flame licked and spat;
Sleek and slender, embroidered in moonlight
Decently approaching in motion, like that of
a cat.

It was then those beautiful orbs collided
In search of hearth they seeped in mine;
Such a scandalous threat they blighted -

In her intensive green eyes did flames
combine.

Slowly as she approached I took her in my
arms
Forgetting the cold as it felt so warm;
Manipulated in thy beauty and engulfed in
thy charms
Oh now that I think, there wasn't done any
harm.

NEW BEGINNINGS

Every part of me craves to hold you in an
embrace
Just like the way you did all those years back.
I came as a part of you unknowingly into this
world
And here you are, taking away a part of me as
I hold my tears back.

Torn away in anguish, I lay my emotions
bare
I know this is the test that we all must face
Yet for that I don't seem to care.

"Thou ow'st nature a death" seems to be
ringing in my ears,
I confide to myself in the fear of losing,
All that I hold too dear.

Death purifies the love corrupted soul in
ways beyond our scheme
For it is not the end here, but the beginning
of a new theme.

A SOLDIER'S WIFE

Always does one wonder
What life holds for thee;
Until he walks the mile and yonder
The pain and suffering that comes to be.

Nobody can foretell the moment -
The line that separates life and death;
For life is all about Peace and War
And death, the pride of one last breath.

But what is this pride
If not a soldier's cry?
Kissing death as one kisses his bride,
Bleeding of warmth as his blood runs dry;

Staring up above at the lofty sky
Tears of farewell stream down his eyes;
Looking at his brother he says Goodbye
For now 'tis the only Truth and no more lies.

Pain and anger, loath and envy
None of that holds any account no more;

For its all forgiven when death draws nigh,
As the eyes searches for the Heaven's Door.

Quenching for some peace at death
As life was all about war;
The soldier draws for one last breath
Exhaling his soul afar.

So often do I inquire why
One needs to wonder and give a sigh;
For life is only a matter of time -
Do not sit idle and let it pass by.

A WILL OF FIRE

The night was stormy
And the room was dark
In between a soul so gloomy
Was not at all lark;

"Quick!" thought suffering soul
As it approached the burning light,
For the lone fire must be extinguished
So that the soul can finally take its flight;

Little did it know that the fire was life
Whose warmth was appreciated by all,
For it was but a freezing night
And without the embers of its life many
would fall;

The fire burnt such a magnificent glow
That it melted even the stone cold soul
Pyres of love gave such a warming blow
The soul couldn't resist the feeling of whole;

The fire burns even through the coldest of
winter

Engulfing in warmth even the ignorant flakes
Tell me now, just like the fire so tender
Can we not play our part without raising the
stakes?

THAT TIME OF THE YEAR

Come away come apart
The snow has finally hit the mart
For the time is nigh when the sledge passes
by
Jingling across our wooden cart.

Trot! Trot! Trot we go!
Dancing on the wet snow
Puffing our hearts out through the smoke
The chilly night makes us grasp our cloak.

The time is nigh I hear the bells
The bells of joy that swells! -
For that time of the year has finally come
When even the Jolly Molly is no more a
bothersome.

You smell the sweet cakes and pies
Where love and care is the main spice
What a jolly festive mood grasps our sight
With all those lights twinkling bright

Lit up your candles, make up your hearts

Make haste make haste the time departs
Make a wish and watch the clock
And don't forget to hang the sock!

SONG OF THE ROAD

Oh what a joy,
what a joy indeed
To love and to lie
Its all a matter of a single deed

Timeless joy, happiness and warmth
Everything at once becoming so vague
Dreams remained onto the scaffolds of
reality
And from this point everything is in vain

Can I be forgiven, O myself
For the countless dreams I've dreamt
The pointless promises which I failed to
keep
I realize now that it's too late

Can I be forgiven, O myself
For the awards that I've won
The talents that I failed to utilize
They remain as showpieces lost in time,
never to be touched by anyone

The mistakes are many in my life I made
Oh how foolish I was to try
To try and try but not try harder
Is the folliest of follies so what's the point to
cry

Was I not brave enough to take the stranded
path
And chose to follow the rest
What I lacked was not courage but sight
Thus I failed to foresee what was for me the
best

I failed to follow my spark of light
Which withered for long in the wild
In the open wind it flickered and went out
And along with it went out my child

Now I'm grown into something I detest
I am everything I once feared to be
So poisonous have I become for now
That I cannot even recognize me.

SCHRODINGER'S CAT

Oh I'll tell you a tale so scary
Of a night in my bed I slept, tired and weary.
And like a gush of wind, it made me thrill
Passing through me, it gave a chill.

Half asleep in my bed, twinkle in my head;
Half awake in my mind, thoughts revolve one
of a kind.
Awake in head, I see the well,
The drowning kitty, and hear its jingling bell -
Too afraid to know what happened next,
It might be alive or dead, but what's the
tingling in my bed!

The eyes they shine so bright as star
Reeking of a poignant feel entwined with
scar,
Glistening stars of emerald and sapphire
Engulfed me in its starry fire.
Jingling-tingling all the way
It finds its place what can I say -
The stare that came aloof,
I was too afraid to have a look!

A look at right as it came in sight
But in spite of all the scanning eye
Tip-toeing through the dark of night
It escaped the surge of dreary plight.
A sense of fear told me to lie -
Still questioning myself: did it die?

Perhaps died it not for then what is this now
Feeling the gaze like that from a soulful cow,
But what if soul it is and the only ghost -
Then it shall come true, what I fear the most.
It was then that I gave a slight bow
And from underneath the bed heard a slight
"meow"!

"Meow-meow" I heard it once, and then
heard it twice
Wiping off the cold sweat with my fingers
cold as ice;
How could it be possible that it was still alive,
I saw it drown with my own eyes, no it
couldn't be a lie -
I tell myself maybe somehow it actually did
survive,
For I am yet not entirely sure if it really didn't
die.

It was then I realised that it had been pouring
cats and dogs outside,
But I feel my kitty moving up and settling
down beside.
Finally I turn to right to hold the creature in
embrace,
That is when I realised something wrong and
in fear I give a raise.
In the dark of night I try to find the matches
and the candle that I seek,
Not able to utter a word, in my astonishment
I've lost the power to speak.

In a sudden thunder-light which for a few
seconds chased away the dark,
I outline a crooked humanoid, sitting and
gazing up like a lark.
Its head hung slightly on the left
As those glistening eyes kept starring at mine,
Like an inevitable force it seeped through me
in my mind as it cleft -
With another thunder that followed through,
its bare teeth gave a shine.

My heart was pounding at the walls
With the humanoid approaching me, as my

mind recalls;
I go numb and stiff to the bone
As soon as I felt its chilled breath,
It was the situation that I cannot condone
As its breath if anything at all, reeked of
death.

All I wanted then was to escape the spot but
the door was so far apart,
And its gaze was as sharp as knife which got
me pinned like a dart.
Behind myself was the only route
Through the huge window which I banged;
But the humanoid came floating close
With its head still tilted like it'd been hanged.

It felt as if my heart pounded my chest open
just as I pounded-open the pane -
For my chest felt so heavy then as if it had
suffered through thousands of pain.
I turned around to my disbelief as the
humanoid was all but gone,
It was then that I heard a call -
And like a lightning thunder it clenched my
neck pulling me through the dark
That's how it all ends as soon as I took the
fall.

I hear myself crashing on the wet ground with
an incredible thud,
That's exactly when I got up and sat up-tight
upon my bed, rising like a bud.
I clasped my hands and squeezed them tight,
As I look around and gave a sigh, wiping off
my sweat -
I realised my cat has been all this while,
purring to my right,
As I caressed it and back to sleep I cleft.

A GIRL WITH BRAZEN HAIR

The Girl with brazen hair, like golden fleece
of the rare
Desired by Pelias the unfair
Upon which the Greeks a million tales do
share.

Cutting edge the shapery, her skin be so fair
Like ivory sheath laden down underneath the
sky so bare.
And when the eyes they blink so keen
A thousand words they mean,
With hand upon my head I say to you, mark
my words
For they're the bravest I have seen.

The braver brow that hovers above
the fearless eyes so fine,
And the tears of life like droplets of fate,
get stuck in the jet black lashes;
Trickles down the cheeks of peaches,
An everlasting brine; -

She's a human divine, in her eyes I see the

shadow of woe and a thousand wars fought;
But still the fire burns in them, in solitude
has she had her peace sought.

The crimson lips that arch on sides
Leaving an aftertaste of life,
Which seems to have produced a smile
To which even the mighty God abides.

The beautiful face held by the slender neck
Upon which a beauty spot remains on check,
Like a sparkling star,
She dives in the ocean of thousand celestial
beings;
Remaining there now and forever, pure in
solitude
Away from the treacherous kings.

MIRRORS

There's something broken inside of me
The sort that's irreparable
Black and blue like a spark of migraine
Aid to which I'm yet not able

Days pass by and life stands still
Like the stagnant water on which lily pads
float
Afloat likewise the false facade through
conflicts
Exaggerations of which come through
minimal boast

Time is fleeting and so is beauty
Like the cherry blossom will it shed its guise
Numerous of petals shall come crumbling
down
Is that sort of beauty worth the price?

Like a child of nature and beauty
Wrapped up in a cloak of joyous mirth
With its slender hands does collect the
bounty
For the Providence has always provided since

it's birth

But I am that leaf, that blossom'd into life
I exist through the innocent observation of
the child
But beauty like life is gone in a blink
No matter how much your passions run
wild.

WHAT A VILE THING

What a vile thing it is,
To go miles without knowing where we're
heading
Or to not question yourself what we are
doing.

To see without seeing
To close your eyes, look away and blink on
the exact second
When the flower is blooming, the stars
shooting, the antlers moving.

What a vile thing it is to not smell through
your ears and hear with your nose
To not know what kind of smell that
symphony has
Or what kind of music do those flowers
compose.

To see just with your eyes and not with your
heart
Touch with your hands but not with your art
To get without knowing how to find

To exist without really knowing anything
about our kind.
To halfburn in the flame of love and not
completely -
Is like to soar high up into the sky without
wings, in a mechanical bird.

What a vile thing it is to drink without thirst
Or breath-in the air of someone you don't
know or desire
To have a leap of faith without being scared
of falling right into the gallows.

To have so much amount of love in you,
more than you can ever spend
Yet like a wealthy miser who's stingy about
his purse
You stretch your arms out to give, but pull
back immediately.

What a vile thing it is to write poetry when
you have eyes to see and ears to hear
A nose to breath and a tongue to fear.
A vile thing indeed it is to be a poet but not a
vagabond,
Someone who can travel to places without

knowing where they're heading
Or what they're doing.

LIES AND DECEIT

In the silence, I tiptoed my way through the
threshold of my sanity Between darkness and
light

I found myself peeping through my senses

Where my eyes failed me, my heart didn't.

What lies above me is Heaven

Always out of the reach;

What lies underneath Is Hell

And somewhere in-between I find myself,
damned.

For the love of God and everything True

What lies we've fed the men:

That in order to have peace, a beautiful smile
on lips spread There must always be
Innocent blood shed.

Where the fields are Irrigated with corpses

And blood feeds the soil;

How can we cultivate peace and happiness

From something so human-devoid?

FLEETING TIME

I see now the world
As it exists through me -
I see now the passion
Which all too sudden has come to be.

From the numerous of living
To the scarce of the non;
Here I stand in the middle
Where nothing but malice is born.

Step by step I walk through it
Weaving my impending deed;
Whilst in the process I undo myself
Questioning my never-ending need.

Many who came are the many who gone
Before and after a few are born;
That life is not what it seems to be -
Unaware and as to the grave they trot
To waste time upon pondering thoughts,
For we in this world have limited time
brought.

ALBERTINE

"I say to you what Swann couldn't
My love is far greater than his for Odette."

If there's ever sun after the rain,
You are that prism from which the rainbow
spreads.
The pallor of your skin so silver and a head
full of gold, makes the ancient gods and
goddesses look old.
Every other color fades and falls to grey
Only when I picture you, flowers of red and
violet bloom on each side of your face.
You must be the sole creature on this
universe,
Richer even than the Gods;
For you have in your possession such beauty
and knowledge
To compare them with you is fraud.

Who else walks the Earth with such authority
but you
Making the snow melt and grass grow anew.
Your smile, the points at which your lips
curve: East and West,

The sun rises at one and sets on to the next.
Your beauty is evergreen, you are the one
who sets the laws of the universe,
The flora and fauna abide by it, and sing your
glory in rehearse.
And the dark clouds that lurk above those
eyes,
That harbor such storms and typhoons I fear!
No sooner did I get drawn to it, a spark,
I'm thunderstruck by your lightening, my
dear.
And when it pours down upon those rosey
cheeks below
Leaving a trail of scattered stars on it's way,
Clustered together upon the starry skies
Like the Andromeda millions of lightyears
far away.

The hardest part of loving you is letting you
go
When all I ever want is to hold you captive;
For you are the prisoner of my heart
'Cause you have committed crimes which I
mustn't forgive.
It must be so wicked of me to even think of
kissing those lips,
To hold you in my arms and embrace you

for eternity,
Oh mankind has forever been a wicked
sinner,
To drink in your smile and smoke in your
breath;
If to sin is to die, then I'll die a thousand
death.

My heart is a mausoleum
For my dreams and passion
My muse, she must be jealous
Ever since I've stopped listening to her
whispers
Her hymns and songs hit hard and bounce
back upon myself, barren -
You make me fall short of words, and
suddenly
All the poems and hymns are but forgotten.

GOODBYE, MY TRAVELLER GOODBYE

Walking through the dusty road
Under the dusky sky,
The sun is 'bout to set
So don't let a moment go by.

Fear not you lonely traveller
Don't stop to fret, don't look aside
'Cause long is the road and short is life
You'll never go astray, long as I'm by your
side.

Look at those shepherds and their sheeps
As they take shelter under the bough,
Not a care they have for where to keep
They comprehend the universe better
somehow.

What do you doubt my lonely traveller
It is unlikely for you to gaze like a cow
Come now, take my hand and don't be
afraid,
For life is a journey and I shall show you
how.

The soft wind kisses you to sleep
As your mind mingles towards the stars
The sun reminds you of a tomorrow
Reminds you of your journey afar.

The water washes you by
As time is running faster than your heart
Giddy up, don't stand still
Stagnation spoils the art.

The rays of the superabundant star,
Melts the snow for greener pasture
Even the highest snowcaps never escape it's
touch
River of tears flow out of rapture.

Mind me not I'm pretty old for this
My bones have begun to tremble
The dead are wiser than the living you see
So silent and so humble.

The scattered leaves and shattered dreams
Of the big old Oak have shed
The time has come when the world stands
still
For the colourful birds have fled.

Under this very tree, darling remember me
The promises you made under the starry sky
Nothing is forever but miles you got to cover
So don't let me keep you long, let's bid
goodbye.

<u>Übermensch: An Epoch lost in time</u>

"The disappointed man speaks - 'I listened for an echo and I heard only praise.'"

In this ignoble existence, I walk alone and long I venture for long I have to go on to cover the distance before I sleep.
What nuisance! - walking alone I realize as I turn around, there is no one talking behind my back.
Where are you O criticizers for if you have abandoned your post who shall take your place?
For how can a man go on to exist without even carrying the speck of idea that he might be wrong? - O you criticizers don't let the traveler astray.
What perfectures shall one do in order to restore the sins of time? What noble critics shall we bring forth to comment on our very deeds? What generation shall we produce to compensate and suffer for the sake of our own sins? - as we suffer for the sins of our predecessors!
What nobility shall we raise them in where we only know too well that Overman is a

distinct and vague epoch lost in time? Isn't
the deed of our very thought of surpassing
the current man, in itself too far fetched that
we have to long to become the Übermensch?
Assuming we will become the Übermensch -
what next? What majority shall we slay? what
genocide shall we display in order to bring
such a drastic change? What more sins do we
need to add on our already blood stained
hands in order to bring forth that which is
being prophesied of? The chosen lamb gets
off the nook, but what about the rest of the
herd - the sinners, the deceivers, the
pranksters, mockers - what of them? Is not
that just another prophecy a much ordained
one this time, and self exhilarating?
Is not the point of becoming a Superman, an
Overman in itself not a cliché - for how can a
man overcome himself when the curse
doesn't even lie in his deeds, but in his belly?
How can a man become god with a belly that
shouts, screams and leaves him overturned!
Such trivialities, such blasphemy - weren't
they also prophesized long before?
As long as man feels hunger, dread, fright,
love, jealous, greed, lust, wrath and pride - he
can never overcome himself. Even the

greatest of great man was human, all too human. And a man without any of that is in all true sense not a man, but an Übermensch - still a concept of man.

(Inspired by Friedrich Nietzsche's *Thus Spoke Zarathustra*)